I CAN'T REMEMBER TO FORGET YOU

Sofia J. Ross

Preface

"I can't remember to forget you" by Sofia J Ross is a book that explores the themes of pain, love, abandonment, and healing. It goes beyond a simple collection of prose and poetry, offering a complete experience of femininity. The author invites readers to confront the difficult moments of life through poetry, revealing that goodness is everywhere, if one opens up to see it. Sofia J Ross's words are raw, moving, light, and unsettling, deeply touching the hearts of those who seek comfort and courage in the power of poetry and sincerity. "I can't remember to forget you" is an honest poem that narrates the daily and collective experiences of contemporary femininity, a work that every woman should keep close to her as a precious companion. It is an invitation to celebrate femininity, to find solace in the sharing of experiences, and to discover the beauty and strength within one's authentic self.

Take this book in your hands as a precious gift, like a traveling companion that supports you along the path to healing. Let the words resonate deep within your being and guide you towards a new positive light, inspiring you to rise again, to believe in love once more, and to discover the wonder of a heart that opens itself to the possibility of loving again.

I can’t remember to forget you...

Love yourself enough
to make the decision
to leave
when you no longer receive
the respect
you deserve.

I can’t remember to forget you

There is a sea
of tears
hidden behind
my smile.

An invisible
yet deep pain
that drowns
my heart.

Please,
don’t misunderstand me
if I stop searching for you.

It doesn’t mean I don’t care,
on the contrary, I care too much.

But I can’t suffer like this anymore,
it’s time to think about my own life.

Yes, I forgot about you,
but sometimes
I still think of you.

Sometimes,
like *always*.

There are small things about you,
seemingly insignificant,
that I will never forget.

Those things
that may seem like nothing,
yet remain stronger
than anything else.

I can't remember to forget you

I wish you could see me
when I come home in the evening
and desperately try
not to think of you,
to forget you,
to erase you from my mind,
failing miserably
every single time.

I've eliminated you
from my life,
but you're the one
who handed me the *loaded gun.*

The problem is not your absence,
but the absence of what
we were together,
the lack of us.

Together, we were
something unique,
unfortunately, *irreplaceable.*

Why does love
last so little,
while forgetting
takes so long?

It's so strange,
after a thousand promises,
a thousand beautiful words,
a thousand kisses,
a thousand hugs,
a thousand gazes,
and a thousand butterflies in the stomach,
to utter five words:

I don't love you anymore.

The saddest thing
in this world
is loving someone
who no longer
loves you.

When it breaks,
it struggles to heal,
and even when it does heal
and starts beating again,
it doesn't beat the same way as before.

The heart is a resilient yet fragile organ.

I can’t remember to forget you

I deleted your number,
yet I know it by heart.

I erased your messages,
but I remember everything you wrote.

We don’t talk anymore,
but I will never forget the sound of your voice.

We don’t hug anymore,
but your scent lingers on my clothes.

Every moment we shared,
I relive them every night in my *dreams.*

I couldn’t trust you anymore,
every time you would leave,
only to come back promising
you wouldn’t do it again.

This time, I prefer to say
adieu.

I don't believe
in people who come back.
I only believe
in those who *stay*.

Time reveals everything.

It’s not important who says
they’ll be with you,
but who remains by your side
when everyone else
has left.

I felt wrong,
I changed everything about myself
just to please you,
I felt like I wasn't enough,
until I realized
too late
that the one who was *wrong*
was *you*.

I can't remember to forget you

I spent an entire summer longing for you,
hoping you would notice
my glances,
my smiles,
then one evening at the beach,
I saw you with her,
my heart froze,
it felt like winter
in the midst of august.

You are admirable
because you are not
the mirror
of what has been
done to you.

Revenge,
an empty illusion.

Heal,
cover your wounds with love and patience.

Keep moving forward,
don't let pain or darkness drag you back.

Don't allow those who hurt you
to influence your future or
shape your essence.

Don't let yourself be corrupted,
don't become like them,
be yourself,
be better,
shine.

We've been apart for almost a year,
a year without seeing you,
trying not to think of you,
to forget you,
but everything
brings me back to you.

We parted ways in the worst possible manner.

We don't see each other anymore,
we don't talk anymore.

But in the places we've been,
it's still the two of us...

The only person
I lost
and needed
was *myself.*

I can't remember to forget you

Since you left me,
everything is more difficult,
I thought I would be stronger,
able to start anew,
but I can't,
because everywhere I go,
I keep seeing you in others,
in their smiles,
in their gazes,
in their mannerisms,
I find a hint of you
in every person
I meet.

I suffered so much for you,
you left me suddenly.

But I'm sure that
one day, when you least expect it,
out of nowhere,
you will miss me.

On a Sunday morning,
you will reminisce about us
and what we were together,
and you will feel a sudden emptiness
in your stomach,
you will want back
what was yours and you let go.

You will long to return to me,
but *I won't be there*.

Listen to the wind,
if it carries my name with it,
for in its whispers,
I find yours.
It was not foreseen,
that our paths would diverge like this,
it was an unparalleled bond.

We deserve another chance together.

You should be free to fall in love.

Fall in love with someone
with whom you can be vulnerable
without having to guard yourself.

You left me here,
in the sands of time,
a shadow of a love
fading in the wind.

Unspoken words,
lost gazes,
the deep silence
of a suspended destiny.

Regret on the lips,
torment in the hearts,
promises shattered
in the night of time.

You left me here,
amongst the fragments of the heart,
still searching for answers,
still searching for love.

I know exactly that you have
your own place where you hide
when everything seems too much, too hard.

I would like to be a part
of that place someday.

I can't remember to forget you

My fear was losing you,
and so, *I lost you*,
like a fragile petal in the wind,
brushing the ground and fading away.

In the darkness of the night,
I still think of you and feel you,
hoping that one day,
I can have you back in my arms.

But for now, all I have is regret,
because my fear was losing you,
and so, *I lost you*.

I believe that sometimes
beautiful things end
so that better things
can come along.

Or at least,
I like to think so.

At the end of the story,
we both lost:
I lost time,
and you lost *me*.

I am accompanied by this strange sensation,
I no longer expect anything from others.

I'm not sure if it comforts me
or makes me a lifeless soul,
if it does me good
or leaves me empty inside.

I believe that no one is so busy
that they cannot be with you,
if they truly desire to be.

If they genuinely want to,
they will find a way
and show it to you.

If they don’t,
let it go
because it means
they *don’t want you.*

The rest are just
pointless *excuses.*

Don't be afraid of losing people.

Be afraid of losing yourself
while trying to please everyone.

Your love for me
was like a warm embrace
that chased away the cold from my soul,
a light that dispelled
the shadows on my path,
a compass that brought me back home,
in every moment.
In every instant,
your love was always here,
ready to warm me,
to enlighten me,
to find me.

Now it's cold and dark here...

Let people lose you,
without trying to prove your worth,
because those who truly appreciate you
will know how to recognize it.

Just because you have
a kind and gentle heart
doesn’t mean
that others
should take advantage of it.

Even if you think
you have everything
you want,
be certain that just before
falling asleep,
you’ll think about the one thing
you truly desire
and don’t have.

You swore you would become better,
You said you wouldn’t make me suffer,
You promised you could never
love anyone else.

You lied.

Before you go back to them,
I just want you to remember
how much they made you suffer while
all you asked for was love.

Is it still worth it?

I can't remember to forget you

Even today,
after all these years,
I forget to *breathe*
when I see you.

If they’re not doing anything
to hold onto you,
then why are you fighting to stay?

It's the most painful thing
to keep loving you
even though you shattered
my heart into a thousand pieces.

It's a thousand pieces of *heart*
that continue to love you,
and it hurts a thousand times more.

I have a *big heart*,
and sometimes I hate it,
I *overthink*,
apologize too much,
forgive too easily,
worry too much
about people who
don't care about me,
I feel *guilty*
for things I
have no control over,
and I feel lonely
because I'm *afraid*
I won't find anyone
who loves me
as deeply as *I love*.

Cry, sweet soul, let go of the burden,
cry, like dew touching the burning ground,
cry, and embrace your sadness with courage,
cry, for every tear is a step towards relief,
cry, and find strength in your tears,
cry, releasing the anguish your heart still holds,
cry, until tears become rivers of healing,
cry, until your soul can finally smile.

Love yourself so much
that you no longer allow
anyone to make you feel wrong.

Love yourself!

I abandoned *jealousy*
when I realized
that everyone is free
to go wherever they want
and to lose
what they want to *lose*.

That girl has changed now,
her aura is different,
a new light in her eyes,
she feels special
because after so much suffering,
finally,
she has decided to choose
herself.

Some things are beautiful
simply for what they are,
not for what they could become.

They are beautiful there, suspended, untouched,
like a work of art
without flaws or blemishes.

The best revenge
is the absence of revenge itself.

Don’t become like
those who have hurt you,
continue on your path
and let *healing* take place.

In loving you,
I embraced the deepest pain,
until one day
I asked myself:

"Why am I destroying myself
for someone who
doesn't want me?"

And the pain vanished...

Perhaps it wasn't written
in our destinies,
an eternal bond between us,
so different,
but I don't regret anything,
because I loved
without fear,
without boundaries.

I can’t remember to forget you

Meeting you
has never been a regret,
but loving you beyond measure,
hoping that one day
you could change,
that was the biggest mistake
I ever made.

Love has disappointed me
so many times that now
I’ve lost count.

But the disappointment
that has hurt me
more than any other
has been
not loving
myself.

Have you ever had to say
goodbye to someone
but deep inside you
there was a
crying voice
screaming
stay?...

You broke the heart
of the girl
who loved you
more than she
will ever love
herself.

Hello, my heart,
I just want to *apologize*,
for all the times
I made you suffer.

Stop dwelling on what went *wrong*
and start focusing on what could go *right*.

How could you let me
open up my heart to you,
knowing that in the end
you would *leave*?

It's not the fear of pain
that scares me,
but the fear of not even
feeling that anymore,
the sensation of being
emotionally numb,
like an empty shell,
without latent sensitivity.

I believe that you
never truly loved me,
because if you did,
you would be here
by my side.

But you're not here,
and maybe now,
you're happy with
someone else.

If I think about how
in love I was with you,
I feel a bit ashamed.

I'm ashamed because what
I loved wasn't really you,
but a better version of you
that I had constructed in my mind.

And when I realized that you were
just like everyone else,
I felt sorry for myself because
I loved the man *you will never be...*

I’m certain
that she will never look at you
the way I used to.

I had eyes
only for you,
my heart
belonged to you alone.

And when
you realize it,
you’ll want to come back
to me.

But it will be
too late.

Sometimes I still find myself
opening WhatsApp
and rereading our
old conversations.

Sometimes I have the uncontrollable urge
to write to you *"I miss you"*
but then I don't press *send*...

I don't do it because I believe
that missing each other
should be a shared feeling...

I can’t remember to forget you

You know when
I really miss you?

When I want to tell you something,
but I can’t do it anymore.

The worst moment,
before falling asleep.

We haven't been together for a while,
but that damned moment always comes.

My mind takes me back
to the happy moments with him:

when he made me laugh,
when he picked me up
right outside my door,
when he looked at me and smiled,
when he kissed me.

Then I remember the day
he left me
and I cry myself to sleep.

When I woke up,
I thought I’d say good morning,
but then I remembered
we’re not together anymore.

Sometimes we don’t realize
that it’s not love
that holds us to a person,
it’s *fear*.

How many times I've retraced our moments,
reliving them in my mind,
feeling every emotion and thrill
as if they were happening again
in this very moment.

How silently I loved you,
trying to make you understand slowly,
without exaggerations,
because I was afraid you would drift away.

How much fear I had of losing you
from the very first moment we were together.

Do you know how much it hurts
now that you're gone?

Do you know the void you've left
deep within my heart?

But if it's as true as they say,
that everyone comes back
sooner or later,
why don't you come back?

I built walls around me.

Not to keep others out,
but to see who cares enough
to knock them down.

We broke up and
I would have never
believed it possible.

You’ll say it was
my fault, but
we both know
the truth.

It ended because
you didn’t want
to *fight* for our story
like I did.

I can't remember to forget you

Every day,
I find myself
wondering
how two people
like us, who
shared everything
to the point of becoming
one entity,
can now
be mere *strangers.*

I cannot
accept such
a waste of *love*.

I was truly convinced
that you were my *soulmate*.

I believed that this time
it would be different.

I felt the sensation
that we were *connected*
by a higher force
beyond love itself.

I will never be able
to understand how
our story
could *end*
so badly.

I don't care
that you're always with me,
what matters to me is knowing
that when you're with me,
you're *truly* there.

Before being with you,
I didn't think
it was possible
to *miss someone*
this much.

The truth is,
I often feel
trapped,
because I can never
fully describe
what I truly feel.

If you truly loved me,
you wouldn’t have hurt me,
you wouldn’t have lied to me,
you wouldn’t have used me,
you wouldn’t have betrayed me.

And you don’t know what love is,
you don’t know what respect is.

You don’t deserve me.

Weaknesses.
You had none.
I had one:
I truly loved.

Every time
you *kiss me*,
I feel a shiver
throughout
my whole *body*..

You are
every
weakness
of mine.

I was there for you
in your moments of crisis,
I was there for you
when you hit rock bottom,
but where were you
when I needed you?

And now,
certain doors
remain closed
simply because
I have learned
to love myself
a little more...

When you suffer,
you may believe
the pain will last
forever,
but trust me,
it won't be so.

Winter will make way
for summer.

No winter lasts forever.

The worst person to be with
is the one who doesn't want to *love you*,
but also doesn't want to *lose you.*

Time goes by,
but the impact
you have on me
never fades away.

How much time
I've wasted
dreaming
of a future
with the *wrong person.*

And perhaps that’s exactly
what gets me.

Being pessimistic
and already imagining
how it will end.

And still ending up disappointed,
because deep down
I imagined
a different ending.

Sometimes *losing*
what you wanted to *save*
can be the true *salvation*.

Who knows
if you also look
for me in the crowd
when you're out and about..

One day you will love me
as much as I love you,
you will think of me
as much as I think of you now.

One day you will cry for me
as I cry for you.
One day you will want me,
but *I won't want you anymore*.

The truth is,
I loved him more than
I've ever loved anyone in this world,
but it wasn't enough,
and he left as if it were
the easiest thing to do in this world.

Do you know why you can't let him go?

Because, despite the pain he caused you,
he was the only thing in this world
that truly understood you and made you happy.

Disappointment
is that
"see you tomorrow"
that will never come.

People don’t disappoint us,
we are the ones who overestimate them.
They have always been who they are,
it was us who needed to see them as *better*.

Talk to everyone.
Have fun with many.
Trust a few.
Rely on no one.

I owe myself
the biggest apologies
for enduring
what I didn't deserve.

If we had never met and
I saw you today for the first time,
I would fall in love with you.

Again,
despite everything.

Do you know it wasn't your fault?

Do you know you couldn't have done anything
to change that situation,
and that you should have never fought
so hard just to be loved?

Do you know you deserve
to have your needs and feelings respected?

You deserve to be loved,
supported, and comforted
during your most difficult moments
instead of being abandoned.

Never forget it.

You shouldn't beg someone to love you.
You shouldn't beg someone to care about you.
You shouldn't beg someone to talk to you.
And you shouldn't beg someone
to prioritize your relationship.

If they want to, they will.

Don't let people become
a priority in your life
when you are
just an option in theirs.

My fault wasn’t loving you,
my fault was giving up everything,
even myself,
just to experience that love.

You should be proud of yourself
for how you have faced this recent period:

from the silent battles you fought,
to the moments when you fell
but still chose to rise again
and look forward.

You are a warrior.

So do yourself a favor,
celebrate your strength.

I deserve
a love
as strong as
all the pain
I felt.

Printed in the USA
CPSIA information can be obtained
at www.ICGtesting.com
LVHW011121021124
795330LV00016B/1078

9 781803 623979